EXPLORING COUNTRIES

Vietnam

ANITA YASUDA

MEDIA ENHANCED BOOKS

AV²
BY WEIGL™

ADDED VALUE • AUDIO VISUAL

www.av2books.com

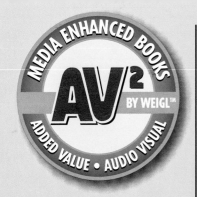

AV² provides enriched content that supplements and complements this book. Weigl's AV² books strive to create inspired learning and engage young minds in a total learning experience.

Your AV² Media Enhanced books come alive with...

Audio
Listen to sections of the book read aloud.

Key Words
Study vocabulary, and complete a matching word activity.

Video
Watch informative video clips.

Quizzes
Test your knowledge.

Embedded Weblinks
Gain additional information for research.

Slide Show
View images and captions, and prepare a presentation.

Try This!
Complete activities and hands-on experiments.

Go to **www.av2books.com**, and enter this book's unique code.

BOOK CODE

K 8 8 9 8 4 9

AV² by Weigl brings you media enhanced books that support active learning.

... and much, much more!

Published by AV² by Weigl
350 5th Avenue, 59th Floor
New York, NY 10118
Website: www.av2books.com

Library of Congress Cataloging-in-Publication Data

Names: Yasuda, Anita, author.
Title: Vietnam / Anita Yasuda.
Other titles: Exploring countries (AV² by Weigl)
Description: New York, NY : AV² by Weigl, [2016] | Series: Exploring countries | Includes index.
Identifiers: LCCN 2015049792 (print) | LCCN 2015050516 (ebook) | ISBN 9781489646156 (hard cover : alk. paper) | ISBN 9781489650290 (soft cover : alk. paper) | ISBN 9781489646163 (Multi-User eBook)
Subjects: LCSH: Vietnam--Juvenile literature.
Classification: LCC DS556.39 .Y37 2016 (print) | LCC DS556.39 (ebook) | DDC 959.7--dc 3
LC record available at http://lccn.loc.gov/2015049792

Printed in the United States of America in Brainerd, Minnesota
1 2 3 4 5 6 7 8 9 20 19 18 17 16

032016
150316

Project Coordinator Heather Kissock
Art Director Terry Paulhus

Photo Credits
Every reasonable effort has been made to trace ownership and to obtain permission to reprint copyright material. The publishers would be pleased to have any errors or omissions brought to their attention so that they may be corrected in subsequent printings.

Weigl acknowledges Getty Images, Corbis, and iStock as its primary photo suppliers for this title.

Contents

Vietnam Overview

Vietnam is a part of mainland Southeast Asia. The country is known for its variety of landscapes, diverse cultures, and unique historic sites. It has many busy and lively cities. However, most people live in **rural** areas around the main rivers. The countryside has tall mountains, lowland areas, and dense forests. There are also many islands off the country's long coastline. Vietnam is officially called the Socialist Republic of Vietnam. Its **economy** is one of the fastest growing in the world. This growth has helped to improve the lives of many of its people.

The Tet Festival, which marks the new year, is celebrated throughout Vietnam.

The Ta Cu Mountain pagoda, or tower with several stories, is popular with tourists visiting southern Vietnam.

Rice, Vietnam's most important crop, is grown in a type of field called a paddy.

At 860 feet (262 meters), the Bitexco Financial Tower is the tallest building in Ho Chi Minh City, the largest city in Vietnam.

Many Vietnamese towns have markets where food, clothes, and other goods are sold.

Exploring Vietnam

Vietnam is a long, narrow country with a total area of 127,881 square miles (331,210 square kilometers). Its shape looks like a large letter S. Vietnam stretches more than 1,200 miles (1,650 km) from north to south. At its widest point from east to west, it is 373 miles (600 km) across. At its narrowest point, the country is only 25 miles (40 km) wide. China lies to the north, and Laos and Cambodia share borders to the west. To the east of Vietnam are the Gulf of Tonkin and the South China Sea. The Gulf of Thailand is off the country's southwestern coast.

Mount Fan Si Pan

Indian Ocean

Mekong River

Mekong River

The Mekong is the longest river in Vietnam and also the longest in Southeast Asia. The Mekong begins in Tibet, which is part of China. It flows for 2,700 miles (4,350 km) through several countries, ending in southeastern Vietnam. The river reaches the South China Sea near Ho Chi Minh City.

Map Legend

Vietnam	Mekong River	Capital City
Land	Mount Fan Si Pan	
Water	Halong Bay	

SCALE

250 Miles
250 Kilometers

China

Laos

Hanoi

Gulf of Tonkin

Hanoi

Thailand

Halong Bay

Cambodia

South China Sea

Gulf of Thailand

Mount Fan Si Pan

Mount Fan Si Pan is Vietnam's highest mountain. It is 10,312 feet (3,143 m) tall. The mountain is part of the Hoang Lien Son mountain range and is in a national park.

Hanoi

Hanoi is the capital of Vietnam. More than 1,000 years old, the city is a blend of modern and older buildings. Hanoi is sometimes called the "City of Lakes" because of its many natural and human-made lakes.

Halong Bay

Halong Bay is located in the northeastern part of Vietnam on the Gulf of Tonkin. In the bay are about 1,600 small islands, with caves and tall stone **pillars**. People do not live on most of the islands.

LAND AND CLIMATE

Vietnam has a varied landscape of **plains, deltas,** highlands, and mountains. The country's lowest-lying regions are the Red River Delta in the north and the Mekong Delta in the south. Between the two deltas, most of eastern Vietnam is made up of a narrow coastal plain.

Mountains and highlands are found inland, in the western part of the country. About 75 percent of Vietnam is mountainous. There are two main mountain ranges. The Hoang Lien Son separates Vietnam from China. The Truong Son range, which is mostly made up of low mountains, is found along Vietnam's border with Laos. A large region of western Vietnam called the Central Highlands borders southern Laos and Cambodia. It is made up of **plateaus** and low mountains.

Ocean winds cause sand dunes to form on the beaches of Mui Ne in southern Vietnam.

Vietnam is crossed by more than 2,000 rivers. In Vietnamese, the Mekong is called *Cuu Long*, which means "nine dragons." This is because the river splits into many branches near the Mekong Delta. The Red River, which starts in northwestern China, is Vietnam's second-largest river. It flows through northern Vietnam before emptying into Halong Bay. Many dams and **dikes** help control flooding on the Red River. Other major rivers include the Huong and the Ka Long O.

Vietnam's climate varies by region. The southern portion of the country is close to the **equator**. This area is hot and humid throughout the year. Northern Vietnam has cool winters. Seasonal winds called monsoons also play an important role in Vietnam's climate. From May to October, monsoon winds blowing from the southeast gather water as they pass over the sea. These winds bring heavy rainfall to all of Vietnam. A dry monsoon blows in from the northeast from November to April. Sometimes, Vietnam is hit by storms that cause heavy rain and flooding. These storms often occur in September and October.

100 Average number of rainy days each year in Vietnam.

2,025 Miles

Length of the coastline of Vietnam. (3,260 km)

74° Fahrenheit

Average annual temperature in Hanoi. (23° Celsius)

In northwestern Vietnam's Lao Cai Province, mountains rise above deep valleys.

PLANTS AND ANIMALS

Vietnam has many types of plants and animals. More than 12,000 **species** of plants are found in the country. They include orchids, bamboo, and woody vines called lianas.

Forests of **mangroves** cover much of the coastline and are also found in the river deltas. The plants' roots are home to small fish, reptiles, and other animals. The Central Highlands have forests of pine trees. During the Vietnam War, which lasted from 1959 to 1975, large areas of forests in southern Vietnam were destroyed. The Vietnamese government is planting new forests.

More than 1,600 species of animals are found in Vietnam. The country has hundreds of types of butterflies. Snakes include the blood python, which lives in coastal areas. Forested areas of Vietnam are home to large animals such as tigers, leopards, and bears. Gibbons and baboons live there, too. New species are still being discovered, such as the saola. This animal is related to cattle but looks like an antelope.

1962 Year Vietnam's first national park, Cuc Phuong, was created.

8 TO 10 FEET
Average length of the Indochinese tiger, which lives in Vietnam and other parts of Southeast Asia. (2.5 to 3 m)

1998 Year the Vietnamese government began a program to plant 19,300 square miles (50,000 sq. km) of forests.

1992 Year the saola was discovered in north-central Vietnam.

The Vietnamese mossy frog is found only in northern Vietnam and China.

NATURAL RESOURCES

Fertile soils, which are good for growing crops, are one of Vietnam's most important natural resources. The richest soils are found around the Red River Delta and Mekong Delta. Farmers grow most of the country's rice in these two areas.

Vietnam's climate and soils have helped make agricultural products one of the country's largest **exports**. Besides rice, other major crops include soybeans, corn, coffee, sweet potatoes, rubber, tea, cashews, sugarcane, peanuts, and bananas.

Vietnam has many valuable minerals. They include coal, phosphates, manganese, iron ore, gold, copper, and zinc. The country has some of the largest deposits of bauxite and tungsten in the world.

Energy from the flowing waters in Vietnam's rivers is used to produce electricity. This type of power, called hydropower, makes up more than one-third of the electricity used in the country. However, the largest portion of Vietnam's electricity is produced by burning coal. The country has large **reserves** of petroleum, or oil, and natural gas.

Natural Resources BY THE NUMBERS

3rd
Vietnam's rank in the world in the production of cashews.

82%
Portion of all farmland in Vietnam that is used for growing rice.

19.1 Million Tons
Amount of coal used in Vietnam in 2014. (16.4 million metric tons)

200 Number of new hydropower plants Vietnam is building to meet a growing need for electricity.

Vietnam has about 300 hydropower plants.

TOURISM

T he history, culture, and landscapes of Vietnam attract millions of tourists each year. The country has many small villages. They offer visitors a chance to see traditional festivals, as well as ancient temples and pagodas. The country's largest cities are lively centers with food and fashion markets, historic buildings, and parks.

The Fine Arts Museum in Ho Chi Minh City contains works from hundreds of years ago to the present day.

France controlled Vietnam for nearly 100 years. Hanoi still has traces of its French past. There are wide tree-lined streets, cafés, and French **architecture**. The Ba Dinh district is also called the French Quarter. It contains buildings from the French **colonial** period. Another section of Hanoi is called the Old Quarter. St. Joseph's Cathedral, a Roman Catholic church built in the 1880s, is found there. It was modeled after Notre Dame Cathedral, a well-known building in Paris, France.

Hoan Kiem Lake is one of several lakes in Hanoi. The Huc Bridge connects a small island in the lake to the shore.

Hanoi's West Lake is a quiet spot in the busy city. Visitors can enjoy the gardens around the lake and rent boats to relax on the water. Vietnam's oldest **Buddhist** temple, the Tran Quoc Pagoda, is located on an island in the lake. Other popular attractions in Hanoi include the Temple of Literature, built in 1070, and Ba Dinh Square. The square is home to the Presidential Palace, the One Pillar Pagoda, and other sites.

Visitors to Ho Chi Minh City, which used to be called Saigon, enjoy its many restaurants, shops, markets, and museums. These include the Museum of Vietnamese History and the Fine Arts Museum. The War Remnants Museum contains exhibits about the Vietnam War.

Scuba divers, swimmers, and sunbathers are attracted to the beaches along Vietnam's south and central coasts. The best-known beach is in Nha Trang. Da Nang, located farther up the coast, also has popular beaches. Surfers go there to enjoy the big waves.

Phu Quoc is an island located in the Gulf of Thailand, 28 miles (45 km) from the southern tip of mainland Vietnam. The island is part of a **UNESCO** world biosphere reserve, or protected area. Visitors enjoy hiking, diving, fishing, and bird watching.

Tourism BY THE NUMBERS

7.8 MILLION
Total number of foreign tourists who visited Vietnam in 2014.

8 Number of UNESCO world heritage sites in Vietnam.

30 Number of national parks in Vietnam.

17 Million
Visitors to the War Remnants Museum since it opened in 1975.

Nha Trang's golden-sand beach is 4 miles (6 km) long.

INDUSTRY

Vietnam's **gross domestic product** (GDP) is about $186 billion. GDP is growing by 6 percent each year. Manufacturing is a major industry in Vietnam. Companies such as Intel, LG, Panasonic, and Samsung manufacture electronic products there. Samsung is the largest foreign employer, with 85,000 workers in Vietnam in 2015. About 16,000 people work in Samsung's smartphone plant in Thai Nguyen, near Hanoi.

Vietnam's textile and clothing industry is one of the largest in the world. Textile factories use raw materials such as cotton to make fabrics. Then, clothing manufacturing companies use the fabrics to make products such as jackets, shirts, and pants. Vietnam also has factories that make shoes.

Nearly half of all Vietnamese workers are employed in the agriculture, forestry, and fishing industries. Some of these workers turn agricultural products into food and other items. The coffee industry in Vietnam employs 2.6 million people. Over the past 30 years, Vietnam has become the second-largest coffee producer in the world, after Brazil.

More Than 54 Million
Total number of workers in Vietnam.

80% Portion of the world's semiconductor chips, which are used in computers, that are made by Intel in Vietnam.

5th Vietnam's worldwide rank in textile and clothing exports.

400 Million
Pairs of shoes Vietnam produces each year.

The textile and clothing industry in Vietnam includes 6,000 companies with about 2.5 million workers.

GOODS AND SERVICES

About one-third of Vietnamese workers are in service industries. People in these industries do not produce goods. Instead, they provide a service to other people. Service-industry workers include teachers, bankers, tour guides, doctors, and people employed in stores and restaurants.

Trade with other nations is an important part of Vietnam's economy. In 1995, Vietnam joined the Association of Southeast Asian Nations (ASEAN). This organization promotes economic and political cooperation among its members.

The ASEAN countries, China, the United States, Japan, South Korea, and the countries of the **European Union** (EU) are Vietnam's major trading partners. This means Vietnam sells most of its exports to these partners and buys most of its **imports** from them. Vietnam sells more goods to the EU than to any other group or country.

Vietnam's transportation systems make it easy for the country to import and export goods. There are major airports in Hanoi, Ho Chi Minh City, and Da Nang. The country has many highways, railroads, and seaports.

The port of Haiphong in northern Vietnam is one of the largest of Vietnam's more than 80 seaports.

Goods and Services BY THE NUMBERS

2007 Year Vietnam joined the World Trade Organization, which deals with trade issues among its members in all parts of the world.

$132 BILLION
Value of goods and services exported from Vietnam each year.

1,616 Miles of railway lines in Vietnam. (2,600 km)

INDIGENOUS PEOPLES

Scientists have found evidence that **prehistoric** people lived at several sites in northern Vietnam. One such site, Trang An, is in the Red River Delta region. Caves in the area provided shelter for people thousands of years ago. Stone tools discovered in the caves date back more than 20,000 years.

Many scientists believe that some of Vietnam's early peoples came from southern China and the islands of Indonesia. Between 3000 and 1000 BC, these people came to the Red River Delta. They lived in small farming villages and grew rice.

The Van Lang kingdom developed in Vietnam around 2700 BC. The kingdom was ruled by the Hung **dynasty**. During the Van Lang kingdom, the Dong Son culture developed in the Red River plains around 1000 BC. People of the Dong Son culture farmed, hunted, and fished. They also left behind large bronze drums and bells.

In the 3rd century BC, the Van Lang kingdom was taken over by a nearby ruler. His kingdom fell in 207 BC to a Chinese general named Trieu Da. He named the region Nam Viet. It included northern Vietnam and parts of southern China.

18 Number of Hung kings who ruled Van Lang.

257 BC Year the Hung dynasty was overthrown.

159 Pounds Weight of a Dong Son bell found at Co Loa, an ancient **citadel** in northern Vietnam. (72 kilograms)

A cave in Cuc Phuong National Park, uncovered in the 1960s, holds tools, spears, and knives dating back 7,500 years.

HAN DYNASTY RULE

Many kingdoms rose and fell during Vietnam's long history. The Vietnamese fought to keep their land from invaders who wanted to control the country. However, foreign powers governed Vietnam for long periods of time.

In 111 BC, troops of the Chinese Han dynasty gained control of Nam Viet. The Chinese occupied what is now northern Vietnam for about 1,000 years. Northern Vietnam came to be called "Annam." Chinese language, culture, and customs were introduced. Also, a new system of government was put in place. It was based on the system of teachings called Confucianism. Education, obedience, and being kind to others were important beliefs.

The system did not benefit most of Vietnam's people, who were poor farmers. Vietnam also was forced to send China valuable goods, such as pearls, jade, and rhinoceros horns. The Vietnamese resented being under Chinese rule and rebelled many times. Finally, in AD 939, one of the revolts was successful, and Vietnam won its independence.

Remains of ancient temples can be found at My Son Sanctuary, in central Vietnam's Quang Nam Province.

THE AGE OF EXPLORATION

In 965, Dinh Bo Linh became the ruler of Vietnam's Dinh dynasty. He built Buddhist temples and monasteries, or centers where Buddhist monks lived and worked. The Ly dynasty ruled from 1009 to 1225. During that time, the country was renamed Dai Viet, meaning "Great Viet." A strong central government was established.

Nomadic tribes from Mongolia as well as other groups threatened Vietnam in the 1200s. They attacked from land and sea. The Vietnamese defeated these invaders.

The statue of an emperor stands in a temple in Hoa Lu, which was the capital of a Vietnamese kingdom in the 10th century.

From 1428 to 1789, Vietnam was ruled by the Le dynasty. Its leaders turned their attention to the south, where there were several coastal kingdoms of the Cham people. The Vietnamese took control of the region. They also claimed the fertile land of the Mekong Delta, which had belonged to the Khmer kingdom of Cambodia.

The tomb of Minh Mang, who was emperor from 1820 to 1841, is found in Hue. Minh Mang was part of the Nguyen dynasty, the last ruling family in Vietnam.

Europeans began arriving in Vietnam in the 1500s to trade and to spread the Christian religion. People in Europe wanted Asian goods such as silk and spices. French settlers soon became the largest European community in Vietnam. In 1858, French troops began to take over Vietnam, and the area became a French colony. Under the French, only a small group of wealthy Vietnamese lived well. Life was hard for most Vietnamese. A movement to overthrow the French began in the early 1900s. One of the leaders of the movement was Ho Chi Minh, a **Communist** who formed a group called the Vietminh to work for independence.

During World War II, Japan occupied Vietnam. After the war, France regained control of southern Vietnam, but Ho Chi Minh and the Vietminh took control of the north and declared independence there. In 1954, at an international conference, Vietnam was officially divided into two countries, South Vietnam and North Vietnam. Soon after, the two countries began fighting each other in the Vietnam War, which lasted until South Vietnam surrendered.

1070 Year that Vietnam's first university, Van Mieu, was founded at the Temple of Literature in Hanoi.

1964–1973 Period when U.S. troops fought on the side of South Vietnam in the Vietnam War.

July 2, 1976 Date when North and South Vietnam were officially reunited as one country.

A parade was held in Ho Chi Minh City on April 30, 2015, to mark the 40th anniversary of the end of the Vietnam War in 1975.

POPULATION

Vietnam has a population of more than 94 million people. The country is densely populated. There are an average of 788 people per square mile (304 people per sq. km). In the United States, there are only 91 people per square mile (35 per sq. km).

Vietnam's population is not evenly divided over the country's 58 provinces. The Red River Delta is the most densely populated region in the country, with 2,432 people per square mile (939 per sq. km). The next-most-populated areas are the southeastern region, where Ho Chi Minh City is located, and the Mekong Delta.

Only about one-third of the Vietnamese population lives in **urban** areas. However, each year more people move to big towns and cities. They come in search of jobs and better living conditions. Ho Chi Minh City has a population of about 7.2 million. Hanoi is the next-largest city, with a population of about 3.6 million.

15th Vietnam's rank among countries by population.

94% Portion of the population under the age of 65.

24% Portion of the population under the age of 15.

Nearly 1 Million

Number of people who moved from North Vietnam to South Vietnam after Vietnam was divided in 1954.

Many cities and towns in Vietnam have floating markets where fruits, vegetables, and other foods are sold. The city of Can Tho in southern Vietnam has one of the best-known markets.

POLITICS AND GOVERNMENT

The country is led by the Communist Party of Vietnam. This is the only legal political party. Vietnam has had a number of written **constitutions** over the years. The most recent was adopted in 1992.

Vietnam's government has three parts, the executive, legislative, and judicial branches. The executive branch includes the president and the prime minister. There is also a **cabinet**. The president is elected by the legislature from among its members and serves a five-year term. The president appoints the prime minister, who must be a member of the legislature and also serves a five-year term.

The legislature is called the *Quoc Hoi*, or National Assembly. It has one chamber with 500 members, all of whom are elected by the Vietnamese people. Almost all members of the National Assembly belong to the Communist Party.

The judicial branch is headed by the Supreme People's Court. This court has a chief justice and 13 judges. There are also various lower-level courts.

The National Assembly building in Hanoi was completed in 2014.

CULTURAL GROUPS

The Vietnamese government recognizes 54 ethnic, or cultural, groups. These groups arrived at different times in Vietnam's history. Each ethnic group has its own customs and traditions. Many have their own language and **dialects**. The Kinh, or Viet, people make up the largest ethnic group. More than 85 percent of people in the country are Kinh. The next-largest ethnic groups are the Tay, Thai, Muong, Hoa, Khmer, Hmong, and Nung. Each of these groups now has about 1 million people.

Members of the Flower Hmong group wear bright, colorful clothes.

The Hmong live mainly in northern mountain areas. They are divided into subgroups, each of which speaks a different dialect. The Hmong are known for their crafts, especially needlework. The Khmer, who live mostly in the south, mainly work as farmers.

The Cham people are Muslims, or followers of Islam. They mostly live along the coast of Vietnam.

The official language of Vietnam is Vietnamese. The three main dialects of Vietnamese are Hanoi in the north, Hue in the central part of the country, and Saigon in the south. Many Vietnamese words come from Chinese. In addition, a number of words were adapted from French. For example, the Vietnamese word *ga* for "train station" is from the French word *gare*. A growing number of Vietnamese people speak English because it is taught in school. Chinese and Khmer are also spoken.

Since ancient times, people in Vietnam have worshiped many gods. Most of these gods were connected with natural features such as mountains or rivers. Some people still hold such beliefs. People also worship their ancestors and celebrate the anniversaries of their deaths.

Vietnam has no official religion, and most people say that they have no specific religion. About 9 percent of Vietnamese are Buddhists. More than 6 percent are Roman Catholics. A small number of Vietnamese are Protestants. Some are Muslims. Some people follow Cao Dai, a religion that was founded in Vietnam.

The Khmer, who are Buddhists, still follow many of the traditions of their ancestors in Cambodia.

6,270 Number of Catholic churches in Vietnam.

1% Portion of the population that follows Cao Dai.

79 Number of mosques, or Islamic houses of worship, in Vietnam.

ARTS AND ENTERTAINMENT

Vietnam has a rich culture and a lively arts scene. Hanoi and Ho Chi Minh City both have performing arts centers, with productions of traditional puppet shows, opera, and popular music. There are also many museums and art galleries. A French painter named Victor Tardieu started the first school of fine arts in Vietnam. Called L'Ecole des Beaux Arts, it opened in Hanoi in 1925. Bui Xuan Phai is often called the "Father of Modern Art" in Vietnam. He is known for his works showing scenes of old Hanoi streets. A group of artists called the "Gang of Five" had a major role in beginning the modern art movement in Vietnam in the 1980s.

Dao Anh Khanh is a modern artist whose works have been shown in Vietnam, the United States, and other countries.

Vietnam is home to many types of music. Traditional orchestras perform using instruments such as bamboo flutes, gongs, and the single-stringed lute called *dan bau*. Ancient folk songs from the Red River Delta, called *Quan Họ Bac Ninh*, are still performed. Many people enjoy listening to pop music by Vietnamese, Korean, North American, and European singers.

The *dan trung*, a xylophone made of bamboo, is a traditional Vietnamese instrument.

Myths and legends are the oldest works of literature in Vietnam. These stories were passed down orally. Later, Vietnamese writing was done using Chinese characters. During the 10th century, a new writing system called *Chu Nom* developed, and Vietnamese literature quickly grew.

The long poem *Kim Van Kieu*, or *The Tale of Kieu*, was written by Nguyen Du in 1813. The poem is about a woman who becomes a slave to help her family. It is considered one of the greatest Vietnamese works of literature.

Water puppetry is a traditional art that is still popular today. It began as a form of entertainment in the Red River Delta when the rice fields flooded. Now, performances take place in cities on small ponds or in pools. Puppeteers standing behind a screen use long rods and wires to move the puppets. A form of folk opera called *cheo* also had its beginnings in the Red River Delta. Folk songs, dance, instrumental music, and poetry are used in each performance.

Water puppetry dates back to the 11th century.

Arts and Entertainment by the NUMBERS

2007 Year the Ministry of Culture, Sports, and Tourism was founded to promote cultural activities and the arts.

67 Number of television broadcast stations in Vietnam.

More Than 20,000 Number of works of art in the Vietnam Museum of Fine Arts in Hanoi.

2,014 Number of cultural and historic sites recognized by the Vietnamese government.

SPORTS

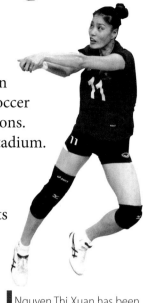

Soccer is the most popular sport in Vietnam, where it is known as football. Vietnam has both men's and women's national soccer teams. They represent the country in international competitions. Their home stadium, located in Hanoi, is the My Dinh National Stadium.

The Vietnamese women's national volleyball team has been very successful. In 2012, the team placed fourth in the Asian Women's Cup Volleyball Championship. It was the team's best showing in its history. In 2014, team members Nguyen Thi Ngoc Hoa, Do Thi Minh, and Nguyen Thi Kim Lien became the first Vietnamese players to sign contracts to play for foreign clubs.

The Ministry of Culture, Sports, and Tourism supports athletic events in Vietnam. In 2015, it sponsored the first Color Me Runs at different sites in Vietnam. Thousands of people, including international runners, took part. In these events, runners are covered with colored powder that is applied at checkpoints throughout the race.

Nguyen Thi Xuan has been a member of the national women's volleyball team since 2003.

Le Cong Vinh, who sometimes wears number 9, is the leading scorer on the men's national soccer team.

Several types of martial arts are popular in Vietnam. One, called Viet Vo Dao, or Vovinam, had its beginnings in Vietnam. It was started by Nguyen Loc in the late 1930s. He saw it as a way for the Vietnamese to free themselves from French rule. The system he created is a mixture of different martial art styles. In 2011, athletes competed in Vovinam for the first time at the Southeast Asian Games. The sport is now practiced around the world.

Taekwondo is another martial art practiced in Vietnam. It was introduced to Vietnam by South Korean troops during the Vietnam War. These troops used the sport to train Vietnamese soldiers in self-defense. Today, taekwondo is a recreational sport. At the 2000 Olympic Summer Games, Tran Hieu Ngan won a silver medal in women's taekwondo. It was Vietnam's first Olympic medal.

Many other sports are played in Vietnam. Adults and children enjoy table tennis. Tennis and badminton also have many fans. One of the top badminton players is Nguyen Tien Minh, who won a bronze medal at the World Badminton Championship in 2013. Nguyen's success is helping to attract more young people to the sport.

Duong Thuy Vi has won a number of medals competing for Vietnam in wushu, a type of martial art.

Mapping Vietnam

W e use many tools to interpret maps and to understand the locations of features such as cities, states, lakes, and rivers. The map below has many tools to help interpret information on the map of Vietnam.

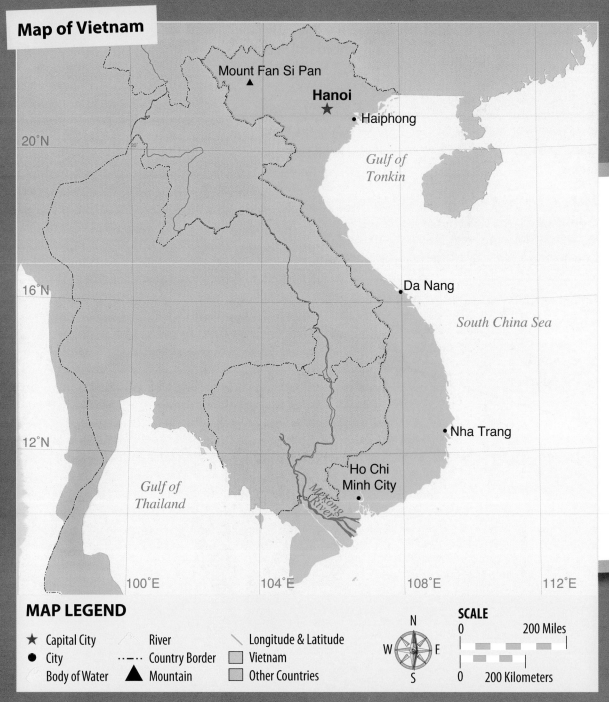

Map of Vietnam

Mount Fan Si Pan ▲

Hanoi ★

• Haiphong

20°N

Gulf of Tonkin

16°N

• Da Nang

South China Sea

12°N

• Nha Trang

Gulf of Thailand

Ho Chi Minh City •

Mekong River

100°E   104°E   108°E   112°E

MAP LEGEND

★ Capital City

● City

Body of Water

River

-·-·- Country Border

▲ Mountain

╲ Longitude & Latitude

▢ Vietnam

▢ Other Countries

SCALE

0   200 Miles

0   200 Kilometers

N W E S

Mapping Tools

- The compass rose shows north, south, east, and west. The points in between represent northeast, northwest, southeast, and southwest.
- The map scale shows that the distances on a map represent much longer distances in real life. If you measure the distance between objects on a map, you can use the map scale to calculate the actual distance in miles or kilometers between those two points.
- The lines of latitude and longitude are long lines that appear on maps. The lines of latitude run east to west and measure how far north or south of the equator a place is located. The lines of longitude run north to south and measure how far east or west of the Prime Meridian a place is located. A location on a map can be found by using the two numbers where latitude and longitude meet. This number is called a coordinate and is written using degrees and direction. For example, the city of Hanoi would be 21 degrees N and 105.6 degrees E on a map.

Map It!

Using the map and the appropriate tools, complete the activities below.

Locating with latitude and longitude
1. Which body of water is located at 19.7° N and 107.8° E?
2. Which mountain is located at 22.3° N and 103.7° E?
3. Which city is found at 10.8° N and 106.7° E?

Distances between points
4. Using the map scale and a ruler, calculate the approximate distance between Da Nang and Nha Trang.
5. Using the map scale and a ruler, calculate the approximate distance between Ho Chi Minh City and the most southern point of Vietnam.
6. Using the map scale and a ruler, calculate the approximate length of the Mekong River in Vietnam.

ANSWERS 1. Gulf of Tonkin 2. Mount Fan Si Pan 3. Ho Chi Minh City 4. 260 miles (420 km) 5. 170 miles (275 km) 6. 115 miles (185 km)

Quiz Time

Test your knowledge of Vietnam by answering these questions.

1 What is the capital of Vietnam?

2 What country is to the north of Vietnam?

3 What is the longest river in Vietnam?

4 What is Vietnam's highest mountain?

5 What portion of the world's semiconductor chips are made in Vietnam?

6 When was the Temple of Literature built?

7 In what year did French troops begin to take over Vietnam?

8 What is Vietnam's legislative branch of government called?

9 Where did folk opera called *cheo* begin?

10 In what sport did Vietnam win a silver medal at the 2000 Olympic Games?

ANSWERS

1. Hanoi
2. China
3. Mekong River
4. Mount Fan Si Pan
5. 80 percent
6. 1070
7. 1858
8. National Assembly or *Quoc Hoi*
9. Red River Delta
10. Taekwondo

Key Words

architecture: the style in which buildings are designed

Buddhist: referring to a religion based on the teachings of Gautama Buddha

cabinet: a group of people who give advice to the leader of a government

citadel: a castle or fort that was used to protect a city

colonial: referring to land outside its borders that a country claims and governs

Communist: a person who believes in Communism, a system in which property and goods are owned by everyone in common

constitutions: written documents stating a country's basic principles and laws

deltas: areas of land near the mouth of a river made by deposits of mud and sand

dialects: versions of a language that are spoken or known only in certain areas or by certain groups of people

dikes: mounds of dirt built to control the flow of water

dynasty: a series of rulers from the same family

economy: the wealth and resources of a country or area

equator: an imaginary circle around Earth's surface that separates the Northern and Southern Hemispheres, or halves, of the planet

European Union: a political and economic organization of 28 countries

exports: goods a country sells to another country or area

gross domestic product: the total value of the goods and services a country or area produces

imports: goods a country buys from another country or area

mangroves: trees or shrubs that grow in swamps with salty water and that have roots partly above the ground

nomadic: moving from place to place as a way of life

pillars: upright supports or columns

plains: flat, treeless areas

plateaus: areas of flat land at high elevations, or heights above sea level

prehistoric: referring to the period of time before written history

reserves: resources still unused

rural: relating to the countryside

species: a group of individuals with common characteristics

UNESCO: the United Nations Educational, Scientific, and Cultural Organization, whose main goals are to promote world peace and eliminate poverty through education, science, and culture

urban: relating to a city or town

Index

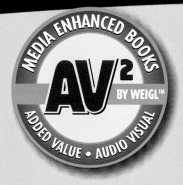

Log on to www.av2books.com

AV² by Weigl brings you media enhanced books that support active learning. Go to www.av2books.com, and enter the special code found on page 2 of this book. You will gain access to enriched and enhanced content that supplements and complements this book. Content includes video, audio, weblinks, quizzes, a slide show, and activities.

AV² Online Navigation

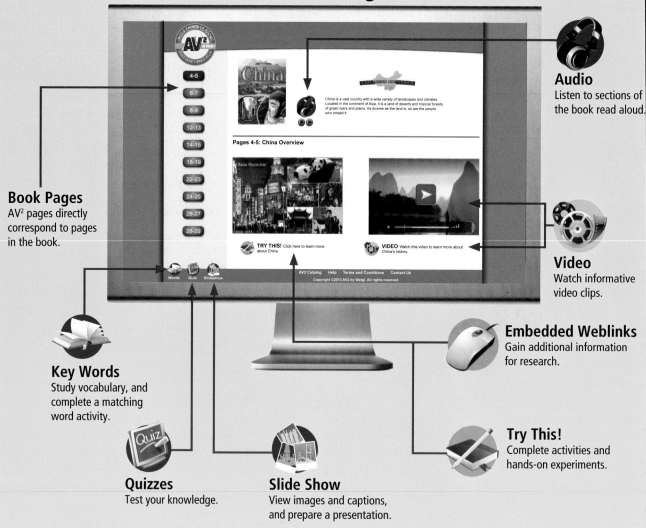

Audio
Listen to sections of the book read aloud.

Book Pages
AV² pages directly correspond to pages in the book.

Video
Watch informative video clips.

Key Words
Study vocabulary, and complete a matching word activity.

Embedded Weblinks
Gain additional information for research.

Quizzes
Test your knowledge.

Slide Show
View images and captions, and prepare a presentation.

Try This!
Complete activities and hands-on experiments.

AV² was built to bridge the gap between print and digital. We encourage you to tell us what you like and what you want to see in the future.

Sign up to be an AV² Ambassador at www.av2books.com/ambassador.

Due to the dynamic nature of the Internet, some of the URLs and activities provided as part of AV² by Weigl may have changed or ceased to exist. AV² by Weigl accepts no responsibility for any such changes. All media enhanced books are regularly monitored to update addresses and sites in a timely manner. Contact AV² by Weigl at 1-866-649-3445 or av2books@weigl.com with any questions, comments, or feedback.